Forget Not!

Forget Not!

Kenneth Hagin Jr.

Unless otherwise indicated, all Scripture quotations in this volume are from the *King James Version* of the Bible.

First Printing 1995

ISBN 0-89276-732-4

In the U.S. write:
Kenneth Hagin Ministries
P.O. Box 50126
Tulsa, OK 74150-0126

In Canada write:
Kenneth Hagin Ministries
Box 335, Station D
Etobicoke (Toronto), Ontario
Canada, M9A 4X3

BOOKS BY KENNETH E. HAGIN

* Redeemed From Poverty, Sickness and Spiritual Death
* What Faith Is
* Seven Vital Steps To Receiving the Holy Spirit
* Right and Wrong Thinking
  Prayer Secrets
* Authority of the Believer (foreign only)
* How To Turn Your Faith Loose
  The Key to Scriptural Healing
  Praying To Get Results
  The Present-Day Ministry of Jesus Christ
  The Gift of Prophecy
  Healing Belongs to Us
  The Real Faith
  How You Can Know the Will of God
  Man on Three Dimensions
  The Human Spirit
  Turning Hopeless Situations Around
  Casting Your Cares Upon the Lord
  Seven Steps for Judging Prophecy
* The Interceding Christian
  Faith Food for Autumn
* Faith Food for Winter
  Faith Food for Spring
  Faith Food for Summer
* New Thresholds of Faith
* Prevailing Prayer to Peace
* Concerning Spiritual Gifts
  Bible Faith Study Course
  Bible Prayer Study Course
  The Holy Spirit and His Gifts
* The Ministry Gifts (Study Guide)
  Seven Things You Should Know About Divine Healing
  El Shaddai
  Zoe: The God-Kind of Life
  A Commonsense Guide to Fasting
  Must Christians Suffer?
  The Woman Question
  The Believer's Authority
  Ministering to Your Family
  What To Do When Faith Seems Weak and Victory Lost
  Growing Up, Spiritually
  Bodily Healing and the Atonement (Dr. T.J. McCrossan)
  Exceedingly Growing Faith
  Understanding the Anointing
  I Believe in Visions
  Understanding How To Fight the Good Fight of Faith
  Plans, Purposes, and Pursuits
  How You Can Be Led by the Spirit of God
  A Fresh Anointing
  Classic Sermons
  He Gave Gifts Unto Men:
    A Biblical Perspective of Apostles, Prophets, and Pastors
  The Art of Prayer

Following God's Plan For Your Life
The Triumphant Church: Dominion Over All the Powers of Darkness
Healing Scriptures
Mountain Moving Faith
Love: The Way to Victory
Biblical Keys to Financial Prosperity
The Price Is Not Greater Than God's Grace (Mrs. Oretha Hagin)

MINIBOOKS (A partial listing)

* The New Birth
* Why Tongues?
* In Him
* God's Medicine
* You Can Have What You Say
* Don't Blame God
* Words
  Plead Your Case
* How To Keep Your Healing
  The Bible Way To Receive the Holy Spirit
  I Went to Hell
  How To Walk in Love
  The Precious Blood of Jesus
* Love Never Fails
  How God Taught Me About Prosperity

BOOKS BY KENNETH HAGIN JR.

* Man's Impossibility — God's Possibility
  Because of Jesus
  How To Make the Dream God Gave You Come True
  Forget Not!
  God's Irresistible Word
  Healing: Forever Settled
  Don't Quit! Your Faith Will See You Through
  The Untapped Power in Praise
  Listen to Your Heart
  What Comes After Faith?
  Speak to Your Mountain!
  Come Out of the Valley!
  It's Your Move!
  God's Victory Plan

MINIBOOKS (A partial listing)

* Faith Worketh by Love
* Seven Hindrances to Healing
* The Past Tense of God's Word
  Faith Takes Back What the Devil's Stolen
    How To Be a Success in Life
  Get Acquainted With God
    Unforgiveness
  Ministering to the Brokenhearted

*These titles are also available in Spanish. Information about other foreign translations of several of the above titles (i.e., Finnish, French, German, Indonesian, Polish, Russian, etc.) may be obtained by writing to: Kenneth Hagin Ministries, P.O. Box 50126, Tulsa, Oklahoma 74150-0126.

Contents

1. Forget Not All of God's Benefits 1

2. Forget Not Your Redemption From Destruction 13

3. Forget Not God's Spiritual Renewals 25

Chapter 1
Forget Not
All of God's Benefits!

Bless the Lord, O my soul, and FORGET NOT ALL HIS BENEFITS:

Who FORGIVETH ALL THINE INIQUI-TIES; who HEALETH ALL THY DISEASES;

Who REDEEMETH THY LIFE FROM DESTRUCTION; who CROWNETH THEE WITH LOVINGKINDNESS and TENDER MERCIES;

Who SATISFIETH THY MOUTH WITH GOOD THINGS; so that THY YOUTH IS RENEWED LIKE THE EAGLE'S.

— Psalm 103:2-5

Do you want to live in the fullness of what God has provided for you in Jesus Christ? Then you'll have to do what Psalm 103:2 says: Forget not all of God's benefits!

You see, the blessings you don't know about or the ones you forget about are the blessings you won't enjoy.

And if you're not enjoying all the blessings God has for you right now, there are probably two reasons why

1

you aren't. Either you don't know about His blessings and benefits, or you're forgetting to act on God's Word concerning them. Those are the two main reasons why God's blessings aren't manifested in believers' lives.

God's Word is full of blessings for you. But the only way to take advantage of those benefits is to find out what God's Word has to say about them and believe His promises are true. Then you must continually remember to act on those promises in your everyday life.

It's the same way in the natural world. For instance, if you went to work for a company, the personnel manager would probably give you a rundown of your employee benefits. But you could leave that office and begin working on your new job and forget all about the company benefits that belong to you.

If you forget about your employee benefits, you won't be able to enjoy them. For example, as time passes, another employee may ask you, "Why did you take a day off without pay? You could have gotten that day off with pay."

You might ask, "What? Are you sure?"

"Yes, don't you remember? They told you about that benefit when they hired you."

When someone reminds you about the benefit you forgot, it jogs your memory. But because you'd forgotten about it, you hadn't been enjoying that particular privilege — even though it belongs to you.

Believers do the same thing. All too often we forget about the benefits that belong to us in Christ. All of God's wonderful benefits belong to us because they were secured for us by Jesus Christ in His redemptive work on the Cross of Calvary.

Everything we have in Christ, everything we receive from God, every benefit given to us by God — has already been provided for us by Jesus. All of God's blessings belong to us now. But we will have to learn how to take advantage of what belongs to us before it will benefit us.

Forget Not God's Forgiveness

What are our benefits in God that we should forget not? Some of these wonderful benefits of our salvation are listed in Psalm 103.

> **PSALM 103:2,3**
> **2   Bless the Lord, O my soul, and FORGET NOT ALL HIS BENEFITS:**
> **3   WHO FORGIVETH ALL THINE INIQUITIES. . . .**

Number one, we need to forget not God's forgiveness. The Bible says He forgives all of our iniquities — not just a few.

Some people live their daily lives dwelling on their past failures, mistakes, and sins. Have you ever met anyone like that?

A person who is always dwelling on past failures can't receive all the benefits God has for him right now because he is forgetting that he's already been forgiven. Therefore, he never really lives free from condemnation.

Suppose you failed God in the past. You messed up. Well, it's true that happened; you can't change the past. But your past mistake doesn't need to dictate your future. Besides, if you've asked for God's forgiveness, He has forgiven you, and as far as He is concerned, that past sin doesn't exist anymore.

So instead of dwelling on your past, forget not God's love and mercy! Forget not His forgiveness! Forget not that when God forgives, He forgets.

> **JEREMIAH 31:34**
> **34 . . . for they shall all know me, from the least of them unto the greatest of them, saith the Lord: for I WILL FORGIVE THEIR INIQUITY, and I WILL REMEMBER THEIR SIN NO MORE.**

Jeremiah 31:34 says that when God forgives your iniquities, your failures, and your past mistakes, He will not remember those sins against you anymore.

Since God forgets your past sins, why should you dwell on them? A past mistake that has been covered by the blood of Jesus is one thing you can forget!

I've actually heard some people say, "I'd really like to get out and work for God, but I've been such a miserable failure. I'm just fortunate that God even loves me!"

People who talk like that have been deceived by the devil into talking that kind of junk! Yes, that kind of talk is trash! Talking that way will rob believers of all the benefits that belong to them. It will only tear down their faith, not build them up in faith or edify them.

Forget not God's forgiveness! Yes, the devil will try to bring up your past and your mistakes to you. But stand your ground on the Word.

Tell the devil, "Listen, Mr. Devil! Those past sins have been forgiven and forgotten. You are the only one who has a list of them, and your list is no good! I refuse to forget God's forgiveness!"

There's not one thing you've done that God won't forgive you for if you ask Him to. But, you see, many people want to categorize sin on a scale from 1 to 10. They seem to think God will forgive the little sins, but not the big ones.

For example, we humans seem to think that there are sins that are somehow categorized from numbers 1 to 10 in seriousness. Then there are even some sins that are only a "5" or fall somewhere in between.

Now if you commit a little sin that's only rated as a "1," that isn't too bad, so don't worry about it. But if you commit a big sin that's rated as a "10" — you are really in trouble! Committing a big sin means you're really a bad person!

People may not say that, but that's what they mean when they say things like, "It's worse if you commit an immoral sin than if you just tell a lie."

You even hear people say, "Oh, but it's all right to tell just a little untruth." But I read in my Bible that God hates lying just as much as He does any other sin! As far as God is concerned, sin is sin (Rev. 21:8).

All sin is transgression! Do you know what the Word of God says? It says, *"For whosoever shall keep the whole law, and yet OFFEND IN ONE POINT, he is GUILTY OF ALL"* (James 2:10).

You see, with God there are no little sins, middle-sized sins, and big sins. If you transgress, that is sin.

But the Bible also says, *"If we confess our sins, he is faithful and just to forgive us our sins, and to cleanse us from all unrighteousness"* (1 John 1:9). That wasn't written to sinners; it was written to Christians. God is a big God, and He can forgive big sins just like He can little ones! So forget not God's forgiveness.

However, if you are unsaved, you need to come and ask Jesus into your heart so He can forgive you of all sin. You can be born again and become a new creature in Christ.

Like the old hymn says: "There is a fountain filled with blood drawn from Emmanuel's veins; and sinners, plunged beneath that flood, lose all their guilty stains."[1]

Once you have confessed your sins to the Lord, as far as He is concerned, your past doesn't exist anymore. God cleanses you from all of sin's guilty stains!

I don't care how bad you thought you were or how good you thought you were — no matter how much you think you've messed up, God forgives you when you ask Him to!

Many times it's harder for the good, moral person who thinks he hasn't done anything wrong in life to get saved than it is for the person who knows he's really messed up and made mistakes in life. Sometimes the person who thinks he hasn't done anything wrong in life doesn't see his need for a Savior.

But whether you've been a good person or a bad person, if you haven't accepted Jesus Christ as your personal Savior, you're still a sinner. It doesn't matter whether or not you've ever committed any "big" sins in your life — not receiving Jesus Christ as your Savior is sin.

Therefore, forget not God's forgiveness! If you're a sinner, ask God's forgiveness for not receiving His Son, Jesus, as your Savior. Receive Jesus into your heart and begin living an abundant life in Christ.

Forget Not God's Benefit of Healing

Another one of God's benefits we are to *forget not* is healing.

> **Psalm 103:2,3**
> 2 **Bless the Lord, O my soul, and FORGET NOT ALL HIS BENEFITS:**
> 3 ... who **HEALETH ALL THY DISEASES.**

Some believers forget this benefit! Isn't it interesting that many Christians can sing all the catchy little tunes from the cold remedy commercials they hear, but they can't quote one scripture about healing!

Then they complain, "I can't understand why I don't get healed!" But, you see, a lot of people don't get healed because they haven't taken the time to find out what the Word says about God's provision of healing.

They've either forgotten about that benefit or they

don't know about it, so they can't enjoy healing — even though it belongs to them!

Then there are other believers who know all about the doctrine of healing. They can quote Isaiah 53:4 and 5, Matthew 8:17, and First Peter 2:24. But the problem is they aren't acting on those scriptures.

You see, if you are waiting on God to heal you, then you're forgetting to *act* on the scriptures that say He has already healed you!

For example, First Peter 2:24 says, ". . . *by whose stripes ye WERE healed.*" That's past tense! Therefore, you just need to *act* on the word!

Some people say, "I'm waiting on God." But did you know that it's an unscriptural statement to wait on God to give you a benefit He's already provided for you in His Word?

You may have to wait *before* God in prayer about something He hasn't specifically talked about in His Word.

But you don't have to wait *on* God for any of the provisions He's already said belong to you in Christ.

Someone may say, "Well, I'm just waiting on God to come through." But it's not scriptural to wait on God to come through. God already "came through" for you at the Cross of Calvary!

Now there is such a thing as being in a time of transition from the moment you asked God to perform His Word in your life to the time your answer is actually manifested. But that's not passive waiting time.

If you are in faith, you are involved in activity because you're actively believing God. You're not just passively waiting around for something to happen.

Waiting implies passively sitting down doing nothing. But, you see, if you forget not God's promises of healing, you are like James, who said, ". . . *shew me thy faith without thy works, and I WILL SHEW THEE MY FAITH BY MY WORKS*" (James 2:18).

What is James talking about? He is talking about doing something — acting in faith on God's Word — not just sitting down and waiting for something to happen. When you are in faith, you keep on believing God.

Faith is actively standing on God's promises!

We're supposed to be active doers of the Word, not forgetful hearers. Being a doer of the Word is faith in action.

> **JAMES 1:22-25**
> **22** But BE YE DOERS OF THE WORD, and not hearers only, deceiving your own selves.
> **23** For if any be a hearer of the word, and not a doer, he is like unto a man beholding his natural face in a glass:
> **24** For he beholdeth himself, and goeth his way, and STRAIGHTWAY FORGETTETH WHAT MANNER OF MAN HE WAS.
> **25** But whoso looketh into the perfect law of liberty, and continueth therein, he BEING NOT A FORGETFUL HEARER, BUT A DOER OF THE WORK, this man shall be blessed in his deed.

So don't be a forgetful hearer of the Word. Forget not to be a doer of the Word. Keep on believing God so you can receive your healing! Faith is not inactive or passive. Faith is active. Faith is acting like what God says in His Word is already accomplished in your life.

When you're not acting on the promises of God, you're really acting like you haven't received your answer. But the truth of the matter is that Jesus already took care of your answer two thousand years ago on the Cross of Calvary! That means you can receive the answer now by faith!

But remember, active faith has a voice of praise. I believe that if there is any one area in which believers are missing it in their walk with God, it is in their praise walk.

Many believers aren't missing it so much in their faith walk. They know what the Word says, and they're quoting it. But they are missing it in their praise life. In other words, they forget to thank God before they see their answer manifested in the natural realm.

What should you do between the time you ask God in faith for your answer and the time it actually comes into manifestation in your life? That's the time to demonstrate your faith by thanking and praising God for your answer.

One thing you shouldn't do is just sit around waiting. You should be actively staying in faith by praising God because His Word is true and He's already heard and answered your prayer.

You should continually declare, "Thank You, Father, for my answer! You said it; I believe it; and it's going to manifest!"

Now, of course, the devil will immediately try to whisper to you, "I don't see anything happening, do you? Everything is just like it always was. Nothing will ever change in your life."

Be a doer of the Word and rebuke the devil! Tell him, "Mr. Devil, I believe God! God said it; I believe it; and that settles it. I'm not interested in hearing your doubt and unbelief, so get out of here in Jesus' Name!"

People who are missing it in their praise walk don't stand up to the devil like that. How do I know that? Because praise enables you to stay in faith. And when you're in faith, you know that doubt and unbelief are just the devil's lies.

People who don't live in the praises of God may quote the Word. And I'm sure they pray because they're continually asking God for their answer.

But because they're not fortified with praise, they fall for the devil's lies. The devil starts telling them, "Nothing has changed. See, you didn't get your answer!" Instead of praising God for their answer by faith, they agree with the devil! They believe him rather than God's Word.

When they listen to the devil's lies, it weakens their faith until they finally admit defeat. Then they begin to confess their doubt instead of confessing faith! They say, "I guess God didn't hear me. After all, it's been a while, and nothing has happened.

"I know faith is real, and I know the Word is true. But I must be one of those who isn't supposed to receive an answer. I'm probably one of those kind of people who just can't receive healing.

"Lord, maybe I just need to suffer for You with this sickness. Maybe Paul was talking about sickness and disease when he said, 'Be satisfied with whatever state you're in.'

"Lord, if You want me out of this mess, then help me. If You don't, I'll just know it's Your will for me to keep on suffering."

Even though that kind of confession hurts a believer's faith, that's exactly what some believers say to themselves. They start out walking by faith in the Word. But then if there's any opposition, they begin listening to the devil's lies.

Finally, they let the devil pull them away from their stand of faith. Then they don't receive answers to their prayers because they forget to act on the Word. They forget to receive God's benefit of healing that already belongs to them.

But one of the ways to tap into God's wonderful healing benefit is to praise God for your healing *before* you see your answer — just because the Word says you are already healed. That's how you make sure you forget not God's healing benefits!

Forget not that God forgives all your iniquities and heals all of your diseases. Then begin to walk in the light of this benefit, so you can begin to enjoy everything else that God has provided for you.

---

[1] "There Is a Fountain Filled With Blood," William Cowper.

Chapter 2

Forget Not Your Redemption From Destruction

Have you ever searched the Scriptures for yourself to find out all of God's wonderful benefits to you? When you know what belongs to you, you can forget not to reap all of God's blessings.

That's why you need to get hold of God's benefits so you'll never forget them. You see, if you're ever going to enjoy all of God's benefits, you can't afford to let yourself forget about them.

Well, what is the best way to make sure we forget not God's benefits? We need to remind ourselves of them by meditating on them over and over again.

For example, when you get a new telephone number, what's the first thing you do? You probably write it down because that helps you remember it. Then if you're like me, you also keep repeating it over again until you've learned it.

What are you doing when you repeat something over and over? You are putting that information in your mind so you won't forget it.

That's the same thing you do when you meditate on God's Word. And when you meditate on the Word, not only are you putting it in your mind, but meditating on the Word causes it to get way down in your heart so it changes your thinking.

It's the same way with other things we want to forget not — we've got to think about them. For example, probably every one of us remembers the multiplication table. What if someone asked you, "What's eight times eight?"

Without thinking, you'd say, "Sixty-four." You wouldn't have to sit down and figure out, *Now, let's see. Eight times eight is sixty-four.*

You don't even have to stop and think about the answer because when you were in school, you went over and over the multiplication table until it became a part of you. So now when somebody asks you a multiplication equation, immediately the answer pops into your mind.

We know how to get hold of natural things so we'll never forget them. Yet when it comes to the benefits that belong to us in the Word of God, we often forget them. But God's benefits are far more important than telephone numbers or the multiplication table!

That's why the Bible says to forget not all of God's benefits. The benefit you forget is the benefit you can't enjoy.

One of God's wonderful benefits is that God promises to deliver us from destruction. For example, look at what Psalm 103 says about God's delivering power.

PSALM 103:2,4
2   Bless the Lord, O my soul, and FORGET NOT
ALL HIS BENEFITS: . . .
4   Who   REDEEMETH   THY   LIFE   FROM
DESTRUCTION; who crowneth thee with lov-
ingkindness and tender mercies.

Jesus was sent to redeem you from destruction. The word "destruction" means *to be destroyed, ruined,* or *devastated.* But the Bible says that it's the thief who robs, steals, and destroys. Jesus came to give you abundant life (John 10:10).

If you are in Christ, you have authority over Satan in Jesus' Name (Phil. 2:9,10). However, if you don't know that one of your benefits in Christ is authority over the devil, you won't be able to walk in that benefit.

We are to forget not that God delivers us from destruction — even from destructive habits. There is nothing so destructive as a bad habit. I'm talking about all bad habits. There are many destructive habits, including those that most people don't categorize as sin.

For instance, if you have a habit of not eating properly, that's bad for you; it's destructive. God made your body to be cared for a certain way. But some people just want to fill their bodies with junk! Then they wonder why they are sick all the time.

When I mention bad habits, many people immediately think about people who are addicted to drugs or alcohol. But there are other addictions, too, that people don't think about. For example, some people are addicted to prescription medicine.

For that matter, many people are in bondage to all kinds of bad habits. But John 8:32 says, *". . . ye shall know the truth, and the truth shall make you free."* It's the Word of God that brings us freedom.

Jesus tells us that bondage to sin makes us a slave to sin.

> **JOHN 8:34,36**
> **34 Jesus answered them, Verily, verily, I say unto you, WHOSOEVER COMMITTETH SIN IS THE SERVANT OF SIN. . . .**
> **36 If the Son therefore shall make you free, YE SHALL BE FREE INDEED.**

When you fall into sin and temptation, forget not that you are redeemed. Forget not that the Son of God has made you free! You don't have to be in bondage to any habit, sin, or anything destructive! Forget not your redemption from destruction!

When you yield to temptation and fall back into a bad habit, you are forgetting that you've already been redeemed from that habit. You are forgetting to act on the truth and walk in the freedom that already belongs to you in Jesus Christ.

There are some lusts of the flesh that our flesh screams for sometimes that aren't good for us to indulge in. For instance, I know some people who think they have to eat at least two big bowls of ice cream every day! That just isn't good for the body.

Others say, "Oh, my favorite program is on television. I just can't miss my favorite program, no matter what happens!" People with attitudes like that are in bondage! Therefore, bad habits can be a result of getting too much of one thing. It may be ice cream or television — but it's still bondage!

None of us should be in bondage to any bad habit. We should only be bound to the Lord Jesus Christ — in love and reverence.

So in your hour of temptation — forget not that you are redeemed from anything that's destructive. Sometimes an hour of temptation is just when your body begins to crave things that aren't healthy — like the wrong kind of food! That's the time to forget not to act on the Word.

If you are being tempted by any bad habits, instead of yielding to them, begin to declare your faith: "I keep my body under, and I bring it into subjection. I forget not that I am redeemed from bad habits. I know the truth, and the truth sets me free! I can do all things through Christ who strengthens me."

Forget Not You Are Crowned With Lovingkindness and Tender Mercies

All the benefits God has provided for you to enjoy in Christ are yours now. But it's not up to God whether you ever receive His benefits. It's up to you.

What's another one of God's wonderful benefits that we are not supposed to forget? Psalm 103:4 says that we are to forget not that God crowns us with lovingkindness and tender mercies.

That's such an important benefit to remember because there are so many people, even believers, who have been abused physically, verbally, emotionally, and mentally. Because of their past, they have deep wounds and hurts inside from lack of love, rejection, and betrayal. But remember that God said, "I will never leave you, nor forsake you."

> **HEBREWS 13:5 (*Amplified*)**
> **5 . . . He (God) Himself has said, I will not in any way fail you nor give you up nor leave you without support. [I will] not, [I will] not, [I will] not in any degree leave you helpless, nor forsake nor let [you] down, [relax My hold on you]. — Assuredly not!**

So if you have hurts inside you, God is saying to you, "I will never forget you! You can always count on Me. I will never betray you!" In fact, He promised us in His Word that He would never forget us, nor forsake us.

So in the midst of all the rejection and betrayal you may have experienced from other people, remember this: God loves you, and He will always be with you. God will never separate Himself from you. To become separated from God, *you* would have to be the one to separate yourself from Him.

So in the midst of rejection, let the love of God flood your heart! Tell yourself over and over, "The Lord crowns me with lovingkindness and tender mercies." Don't ever let yourself forget that precious benefit!

Now let me explain something that some people don't understand. Faith does not pretend there is no hurt. And faith does not deny the circumstances.

But many people think they are not in faith if they admit the painful circumstances or the hurts in their lives.

For instance, I heard one divorced person say, "Well, I'm just not ever going to confess, 'I'm divorced.' I'm going to say that a divorce has never occurred in my family."

I told him, "It doesn't matter whether you confess that you are divorced or not — it's a fact! Your divorce is already logged down at the county courthouse. Your saying it hasn't happened won't change the facts."

You see, faith doesn't deny the circumstances. But faith looks beyond the circumstances to the Word.

But first you have to face the circumstances so you can know how to apply the Word to your situation. For example, before you could ever be saved, you had to recognize the fact that you were a sinner. But then you looked to the Word and put the Word to work so you could get saved.

In the same way, before you can receive help from the Lord for past hurts, you have to recognize that those hurts exist and that you need to be delivered from them.

Look at what Isaiah 49:15 and 16 says. It tells us that God will never forsake us. No matter what we've been through, God will help us.

ISAIAH 49:15,16
**15 Can a woman forget her sucking child, that she
should not have compassion on the son of her
womb? yea, they may forget, YET WILL I NOT
FORGET THEE.**
**16 Behold, I HAVE GRAVEN THEE UPON THE
PALMS OF MY HANDS; thy walls are continually
before me.**

Because God loves us so much, Jesus Himself bore
nails in the palms of His hands at the Cross of Calvary
for you and me.

This scripture says that God will never forget us!.
And as I put the Scriptures together, I see that no matter who rejects us, no matter what has happened to us
in the past, Jesus Christ Himself loves us with a love
far greater than anyone else's love (Rom. 8:37-39).

The Bible tells us what kind of love Jesus has for us
when it says, *"Greater love hath no man than this, that
a man lay down his life for his friends"* (John 15:13).
Jesus did that for you and me!

So when the devil tries to make you feel bad, look to
God! When the devil tries to get you discouraged and
despondent with rejection and hurt, remember what
Jesus did for you.

Tell God, "Heavenly Father, I'm just going to crawl
up in Your lap and let You put Your arms around me
and love me."

You never have to *allow* feelings of rejection to
defeat you again. I didn't say you'd never *experience*
rejection again from people. Faith doesn't deny that the

hurt exists. It doesn't deny the heartbreak. Hurt and heartbreak are real; they exist.

For example when someone rejects you or when you lose a loved one, it does hurt. But faith applies the living Word of God to the situation! Faith in the Word allows you to rise above your circumstances because true faith won't settle for anything less than enjoying God's benefits!

Therefore, forget not that God has crowned you with His lovingkindness and tender mercies! He is more than able to bring you restoration and healing.

When you know and understand the love of God and His mercy, your countenance will change. No longer will you be sad and depressed. Your whole life will change and take on new meaning.

No matter how people have hurt you in the past, you can look to God, and God will wash away all the hurt. He will restore you so you can walk in victory in your future.

Your Heavenly Father stands ready with open arms to reach down to you right now. He wants to encircle you in His arms, hold you close, and say, "My child, I love you. Nothing can hurt you anymore as long as you stay wrapped in My everlasting arms. Nothing and no one can take you out of My love."

Forget not God's lovingkindness. Forget not His tender mercies to you. Nothing can separate you from the love of God. God promised that in His Word. Even though the storms of life may come against you, God promises to take care of you!

ROMANS 8:37-39
37 Nay, in all these things WE ARE MORE THAN CONQUERORS through him that loved us.
38 For I am persuaded, that neither death, nor life, nor angels, nor principalities, nor powers, nor things present, nor things to come,
39 Nor height, nor depth, nor any other creature, SHALL BE ABLE TO SEPARATE US FROM THE LOVE OF GOD, which is in Christ Jesus our Lord.

As long as you stay in God's love and in His tender mercies, nothing can separate you from the love of God.

Confess this from your heart:

> Nothing can separate me from the love of God! God can redeem me from all the hurts of the past through Jesus' precious blood.
>
> Because of God's great love and the tender mercies He's shown to me, I can be free from all hurts. I'm not saying the hurts never existed. But the love of God can heal every hurt.

Yes, we're emotional people, and we have feelings. But we are also spiritual people, and when we learn how to stand on God's Word in faith, we can overcome circumstances. We don't have to be overcome by our circumstances. We can learn how to let our spirits dominate us so we can keep our feelings in line with the Word.

Every one of us has faced hurt, pain, and disappointment at some time in our lives. Every one of us has known failure. But, thank God, we can forget not that God crowns us with His lovingkindness and His tender mercies! God's love gives us the strength to overcome any disappointment, hurt, or failure.

Chapter 3
Forget Not God's Spiritual Renewals

It is important that you search the Word of God for yourself to discover God's many bountiful blessings and benefits. Then be mindful to forget not that God has prepared each one of them just for you.

Another benefit you should forget not is that God renews your youth like the eagle's. He renews your spirit so that you can be continually refreshed by His Spirit. Psalm 103:5 says ". . . *satisfieth thy mouth with good things; so that thy youth is renewed like the eagle's.*"

One of the wonderful benefits of God is that we do not have to be sick, weak, and tired. We can be renewed! We can be full of life, strength, and vitality.

There is a correlation between renewing the physical man and renewing the spiritual man. The Bible tells us how to renew both our physical strength and our spiritual strength.

> **ISAIAH 40:31**
> 31 But THEY THAT WAIT UPON THE LORD SHALL RENEW THEIR STRENGTH; they shall mount up with wings as eagles; they shall run, and not be weary; and they shall walk, and not faint.

Many people would like their strength renewed; they'd like to go through their days with strength and vitality and not get weary. Well, God promises to renew our strength!

But something comes into play in this verse that we must understand. God is not going to renew the physical man if we have not renewed the spiritual man on the inside.

The renewal of the physical man on the outside comes from within — from your spirit. It does not come from without!

Many people are always looking for the secret of renewing their youth. For instance, they try rubbing creams on their face to look younger. They take vitamins; they try this, that, and the other thing. They're always searching for secrets to renew their youth.

My dad, Rev. Kenneth E. Hagin, has been in the ministry more than 60 years, but he's still going strong. He teaches at RHEMA, Campmeeting, and Winter Bible Seminar and conducts a variety of meetings and Ministers' Conferences around the country every year.

People ask, "How in the world does Brother Hagin do it?"

I tell them, "Dad can keep up that pace because he's learned the secret of renewing the spirit man on the inside with the Holy Spirit."

The Bible says that the same Spirit that raised up Christ from the dead shall quicken our mortal bodies (Rom. 8:11). Our bodies are quickened or made alive by the power of the Holy Spirit!

Praying in the Spirit is also important if you are going to renew your inner man. Paul said that when you speak in tongues, you edify or build up your spirit (1 Cor. 14:4). When you get your spirit man on the inside charged up, it will help to renew that mortal man on the outside!

Of course, there are also other things involved in renewing your youth. You can't expect your youth to be renewed like the eagle's unless you live right, eat right, and take care of your body. That's just common sense.

Also, you'll have a hard time renewing the inward man if you don't keep your mouth continually filled with praise. When your mouth is filled with griping, complaining, worry, and fear, you are actually subtracting from your youth and vigor.

Did you know that you can't change 99.9 percent of the things you complain and worry about anyway? If you could have changed them, you would have already changed them!

So all your complaining is not doing one bit of good. All it's doing is keeping you confused and torn up inside. And it's keeping you from getting your youth renewed like the eagle's.

People can also hinder themselves from renewing their inner man by spending all their time doing natural activities. For instance, Christians should be careful about what they watch on television.

I'm not saying you can't enjoy some leisure time watching television. Just make sure that what you watch isn't putting junk into your mind and heart!

But, really, we can't afford to spend all of our time watching even good television programs. We must make sure we have enough time in the Word. There's a balance between our natural life and our spiritual life that we'll need to find if we want to renew our inner man.

You can do other things to renew your youth too. But did you know you can let yourself get so busy that you forget to do what you know to do? You can forget to do those things that will help you renew your strength and vitality.

For instance, you know you're supposed to read the Bible. You know you're supposed to pray. But you can get so caught up in the affairs of life that you say, "Oh, I'm just too busy to read the Word today. I got up late, and I have an appointment. I'll spend time praying later."

Then you run, run, run all day long. Finally, you get home at night, and the kids need help with their homework. The car isn't running right, so you have to work on it. Then the air conditioner starts giving you a problem, so you have to see what's the matter with it.

By that time it's late, and you have an early appointment the next day. Before you know it, you've taken a shower, laid your head down on the pillow, and said, "Lord, bless us. Thank You." And you're off to sleep! That's not the way to renew your inner man!

Some of you may laugh at that because it describes your typical day! But no matter what your schedule looks like, you need to make time to get in the Word every day. You also need to pray every day in the Spirit to build up your inner man.

When you spend time in the Presence of God, your inner man will energize your outward man by the power of the Holy Spirit. That's how you forget not to act on God's benefit of renewing your youth like the eagle's!

Forget Not God's Benefit of Long Life

How many of you want to live a long life on this earth? Then you must forget not that God has promised you long life.

> **PSALM 91:16**
> **16 With LONG LIFE WILL I SATISFY HIM, and shew him my salvation.**

God wants us to live a long time on the earth to His glory. This is another one of God's wonderful benefits. But did you know that long life is conditional?

Yes, all the promises concerning long life are conditional. Some people won't live a long time on the earth because they're not meeting the conditions.

I didn't say they aren't Christians. I didn't say they don't know how to have faith or how to believe God. I just said they aren't meeting the conditions to live a long life on this earth.

Let's look at something the Lord said to Israel. This also applies to us because believers are spiritual Israel. How do I know that? Because Galatians 3:29 says we are the seed of Abraham. Therefore, in Christ we have become the spiritual seed of Abraham. So this verse applies to us too.

> **DEUTERONOMY 5:16**
> 16 Honour thy father and thy mother, as the Lord thy God hath commanded thee; THAT THY DAYS MAY BE PROLONGED, and that it may go well with thee, in the land which the Lord thy God giveth thee.

If this promise of long life was for natural Israel, it is also for spiritual Israel. If it's for the natural descendants of Abraham — then it's also for us because we are the seed of Abraham.

God also tells us something else we can do to prolong our days upon the earth.

> **DEUTERONOMY 11:18-21**
> 18 Therefore shall ye lay up these my words in your heart and in your soul, and BIND THEM FOR A SIGN UPON YOUR HAND, that they may be AS FRONTLETS BETWEEN YOUR EYES.
> 19 And ye shall teach them your children, speaking of them when thou sittest in thine house, and when thou walkest by the way, when thou liest down, and when thou risest up.
> 20 And thou shalt write them upon the door posts of thine house, and upon thy gates:
> 21 THAT YOUR DAYS MAY BE MULTIPLIED, and the days of your children, in the land which the Lord sware unto your fathers to give them, as the days of heaven upon the earth.

In verse 18, God is telling us to bind His Word to

our hearts and minds so that they may be "as frontlets between our eyes."

God is telling us to put the things that we are to *forget not* right in front of our eyes, so there is no way we can possibly forget them!

Why are we supposed to put God's Word in our heart and soul and bind them on our hands? Verse 21 says, *"That your days may be multiplied. . . ."* God is telling us how to live a long time on the earth!

We are to forget not the promises of God. We are to keep them ever before our eyes. We are to meditate on them constantly and talk about them all the time.

How many times a day do you notice your hands? You use your hands so many times during the day, you don't even think about them, do you?

Well, if the Word of God were written on your hands, you would see the Word every time you glanced at them. You'd really get the Word down into your heart that way!

That's exactly what God wants us to do with the Word. It should be in front of our eyes so that it's always on our minds. If the Word is constantly in front of our eyes, we won't forget any of God's benefits.

Forget not God's benefit of long life! But in order to *forget not*, you will have to remember the conditions involved in enjoying long life. You must be obedient to God and meet His conditions to qualify for His blessings. It's when you act on the *conditions* of God that you reap the *benefits* of God!

PROVERBS 9:10,11
10 The FEAR OF THE LORD is the beginning of
wisdom: and the knowledge of the holy is understanding.
11 For by me thy DAYS SHALL BE MULTIPLIED,
and the YEARS OF THY LIFE SHALL BE
INCREASED.

God tells us another way we can enjoy His benefit of
long life! Godly fear of the Lord and acting on His wisdom bring us long life. When we do what we're supposed to do, then we enjoy the benefits God has already
promised us.

PROVERBS 10:27
27 The FEAR OF THE LORD PROLONGETH
DAYS: but the years of the wicked shall be short-
ened.

The word "fear" in this verse does not mean to be
afraid of God. It means to be in reverent awe of God. It
means to respect God so that you will obey Him.

But this verse also says that when you don't do
what God told you to do, you are shortening your days
on this earth. A lot of people are shortening their days
through disobedience, aren't they?

1 PETER 3:10
10 For HE THAT WILL LOVE LIFE, and SEE
GOOD DAYS, let him refrain his tongue from evil,
and his lips that they speak no guile.

It's evil when you gripe and complain and speak words of strife. It's evil when you go around whispering to others, "Oh, did you hear what So-and-so did? I don't want to gossip or anything, but did you hear about it?"

Not long ago, a person started talking to me about some things, and I just said, "Wait a minute. I really don't care to hear all this."

Then I said, "I don't know whether or not that person really did what you said. But if he did, maybe he's already asked forgiveness for it. But how can that person ever go on with God if people go around telling what he did and spreading it around? That's not right!"

How many of you have been forgiven for something that happened some time ago? All of us have, and we just need to forget about it and go on with God. But, you know, some people just like to gossip, and they talk about other people's past mistakes like they happened just yesterday.

Actually, Christians should do what the Bible says here in First Peter 3:10 and refrain their mouths from evil. If they would just practice this verse, there wouldn't be all the gossiping going on that hurts and injures people.

God forgives! But for some reason or another, some people can't seem to forgive. But then they want to shout, "Glory, glory, hallelujah! God's going to bless me!"

No, He's not! One of the ways you tap into the benefit of a long life is to refrain your mouth from speaking evil. The Bible talks about this in the New Testament.

1 PETER 3:11
11 Let him eschew [avoid] **evil, and do good; let him seek peace, and ensue it.**

We are supposed to seek peace, not strife. Do you know that there are some people who just seem to love to stir up strife and discord? And for some reason it seems that about ninety percent of those kind of people are in the church! It seems as though they want to keep trouble stirred up all the time. But that won't lengthen their days; it will shorten them!

We need to know that there are conditions to receiving the blessings of God! You cannot forget about keeping your mouth from evil and still expect to be blessed.

Forget Not God's Protection

Another one of God's wonderful benefits is His strong arm of protection. But just like other benefits, there are conditions for receiving all of God's benefit of protection. We must find out what His conditions are in order to constantly dwell in safety.

So many believers quote verses on protection. For example, you hear them quoting Psalm 91. But many of them don't realize that for the Lord to be their refuge, they've got to dwell in the secret place of the most High!

PSALM 91:1,2
1 He that dwelleth in the secret place of the most High shall abide under the shadow of the Almighty.

2   I will say of the Lord, HE IS MY REFUGE AND MY FORTRESS: my God; in him will I trust.

The person who dwells in the secret place of the Most High is not going to be griping, complaining, and stirring up strife!

Now I want you to notice some principles about this passage of Scripture in Psalm 91. Verse 2 tells you how to make a good biblical confession. It says, "I will say of the Lord, He is my refuge and my fortress."

Then it says, "I will trust in the Lord!" That is also a good confession to make.

But instead of making good confessions like that, some people confess, "The Lord is my refuge." Then in the next breath, they say, "But, you know, I just can't figure out why God let this happen to me!"

There's no faith in a statement like that! If people only realized they are doubting God with such statements, they wouldn't say such things. But many don't realize that. Then they go on and try to claim one of God's benefits: "Thank You, Lord, for long life."

No, in the midst of the storm, in the midst of the trouble — God is my refuge and in Him will I trust! I'm not going to say, "God, why did you let this happen to me?" when things seem to go wrong. God is not the author of evil — Satan is (John 10:10).

God promised to deliver us in trouble! That promise is what we are to set our faith on instead of agreeing with the devil by making bad confessions.

PSALM 91:14-16
14 Because he hath set his love upon me, THERE-
FORE WILL I DELIVER HIM: I will set him on
high, because he hath known my name.
15 He shall call upon me, and I will answer him: I
will be with him in trouble; I WILL DELIVER HIM,
and honour him.
16 WITH LONG LIFE WILL I SATISFY HIM, and
shew him my salvation.

In other words, if you forget not to set your love on God, then God will deliver you — no matter what you face.

But when you set your love on God, you're not going to be doubting Him either!

You are going to trust Him. God will set you on High — far above all your problems — if you'll just forget not His benefits and confess them!

God says that as soon as a child of God calls upon Him, He hears him. He doesn't say, "I'll hear him if I'm not busy." Or "He's going to have to call on Me a lot before I'll finally answer him."

No, God just promises, "When he calls, I will answer him!" Then in the same verse, God promises to be with us in trouble. That tells me that trouble is going to come to all of us from time to time because we live in this world where Satan is god (2 Cor. 4:4).

But God is not going to ignore us or run away from us when we're in trouble — He's going to be there to help us. That's what God said in Psalm 91:15: ". . . *I will deliver him*. . . ." That includes each one of us!

Not only will God help us, but verse 15 also says that God will honor us when we cry to Him for help. Why is God going to honor us?

God will honor us when we meet the conditions He has established for us. And as we forget not all of His benefits, He will show us His salvation in every situation!

Now let me ask you this question: "How often does God want you to think about His benefits?"

My answer to that question is, "How often do you want to enjoy His benefits?"

Remember, it's up to you whether or not you enjoy His benefits. It's up to you! *You* are the one who has to forget not.

Forget not peace. Forget not long life and God's mighty delivering power from destruction. Forget not God's divine protection and His lovingkindness and tender mercies.

Forget not that God has forgiven you and cleansed you of past sins and mistakes by the blood of His Son, Jesus Christ. You are redeemed by Jesus' blood, so you can walk in all of God's wonderful benefits.

Forget not that by Jesus' stripes you were healed. And forget not that you have been redeemed from every destructive habit that has tried to bind you in the past.

Forget not God's mercy and His lovingkindness so you can walk in His mercy and grace.

What are you doing with the benefits of God? Are you forgetting them? Or are you walking in them?

I have only mentioned a few of God's many benefits. But dig into the Word for yourself and find out what is yours in Christ. Remember that God promised to supply *all* your needs according to the riches of His glory in Christ (Phil. 4:19), so find out what belongs to you!

Do you want to walk in the freedom and the victory that belong to you as a child of God? Then discover for yourself the bountiful blessings and benefits you have in Christ and walk in them!

There's a reason God told us, "Forget not My benefits." You see, God has His responsibility to bring those benefits to pass in our lives, and we have our responsibility to walk in those benefits.

But God has already done His part — He's provided the benefits, and He is always faithful to keep His promises! Now it's up to us to fulfill our responsibility by forgetting not. Then we have to meet His conditions so we can reap the benefits.

All the benefits of God are there for you to enjoy. It's up to you to establish them in your heart so you can forget them not! It's also up to you to do something about receiving them by faith. You can't walk in the benefits if you don't even remember they belong to you!

So remember God's benefits. Keep them always before your eyes. Meditate on them so they're firmly established in your heart. Don't be robbed of experiencing God's blessings by allowing the enemy to pull you away from the Word of God.

Get hold of the Word the same way you learned to remember other truths that were important to you. If you constantly think about God's benefits, you won't forget them!

Forget not all of God's benefits. Act on God's Word in faith, and enjoy the blessings that are yours in Jesus Christ!

Let me share a little secret with you. When you know God's Word and you have meditated on all of His benefits until they are established deep in your heart, then you'll find as you walk according to the Word, you'll begin to *receive* those benefits. And you'll find that the blessings of God will start *overtaking* you as you forget not all of His benefits!